W9-AMP-824

The · Life Cycle · Series

The Life Cycle of a Koala

Bobbie Kalman & Heather Levigne

Crabtree Publishing Company

www.crabtreebooks.com

The Life Cycle Series

A Bobbie Kalman Book

For my beautiful cousin Margaret

Editor-in-Chief
Bobbie Kalman

Writing team
Bobbie Kalman
Heather Levigne
Kathryn Smithyman

Editors
Amanda Bishop
Niki Walker

Cover design
Campbell Creative Services (front)
Kymberley McKee Murphy (back)

Computer design
Margaret Amy Reiach

Production coordinator
Heather Fitzpatrick

Photo researcher
Heather Fitzpatrick

Consultant
Patricia Loesche, Ph.D., Animal Behavior Program,
Department of Psychology, University of Washington

Photographs
©Erwin and Peggy Bauer: pages 13, 14, 15 (top right), 16,
    20, 21, 31
©Gerry Ellis/GerryEllis.com: front cover
©C. Andrew Henley-Larus: title page, pages 4, 12,
    15 (top left and bottom), 18, 19, 22, 23 (right),
    25, 26, 27 (top right)
©Wolfgang Kaehler: page 29
Tom Stack and Associates: Dave Watts: pages 23 (left),
    24 (bottom);
    Peter Mead: page 27 (bottom)
www.koala.net: page 11
Other images by Digital Stock

Illustrations
Barbara Bedell: series logo, back cover (center), pages 5,
    6-7 (koalas), 9 (top and bottom), 22
Margaret Amy Reiach: cover borders, pages 3, 8, 9 (left), 16
Bonna Rouse: pages 9 (right), 10, 11
Tiffany Wybouw: all leaf borders, 6-7 (map), 26-27

Crabtree Publishing Company

www.crabtreebooks.com   1-800-387-7650

PMB 16A	612 Welland Avenue	73 Lime Walk
350 Fifth Avenue	St. Catharines	Headington
Suite 3308	Ontario	Oxford
New York, NY	Canada	OX3 7AD
10118	L2M 5V6	United Kingdom

Cataloging in Publication Data
Kalman, Bobbie
    The life cycle of a koala / Bobbie Kalman & Heather Levigne.
    p. cm. -- (The life cycle)
    Includes index.
    Describes the physical characteristics, behavior, life cycle,
and natural environment of the koala, a marsupial found only
in Australia.
    ISBN 0-7787-0655-9 (RLB) -- ISBN 0-7787-0685-0 (pbk.)
    1. Koala--Life cycles--Juvenile literature. [1. Koala.]   I.
Levigne, Heather. II. Title.
    QL737.M384 K35 2002
    599.2'5--dc21
                                            2001047104

Contents

What is a koala?

Koalas are **mammals**. Mammals are **warm-blooded** animals. Their bodies stay the same temperature no matter how warm or cold their surroundings are. Mammals have backbones and some hair or fur on their bodies. Female mammals make milk in their bodies to feed their babies. Koalas are also **marsupials**, or mammals with pouches.

Growing in a pouch

Most baby mammals **gestate**, or grow inside the bodies of their mothers, until they are ready to be born. A marsupial baby is different from other mammal babies. It grows inside its mother's body for only a short time. The tiny baby then moves to a pouch on its mother's abdomen, where it drinks milk and finishes growing.

Koala relatives

Kangaroos, Tasmanian devils, wombats, and cuscuses are also marsupials. They have different body types, diets, and homes, but every marsupial begins life in the same way. Each develops inside a pouch on its mother's body.

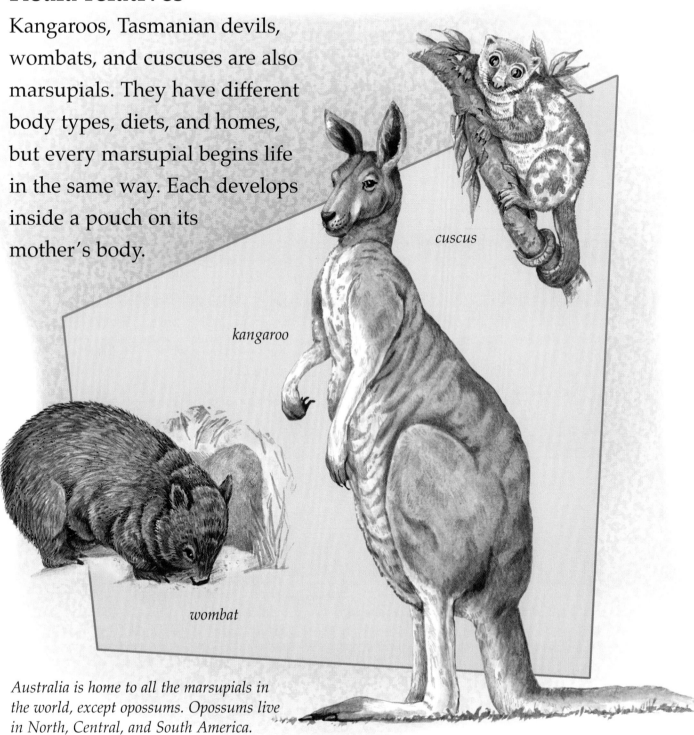

cuscus

kangaroo

wombat

Australia is home to all the marsupials in the world, except opossums. Opossums live in North, Central, and South America.

Where do koalas live?

Koalas live in Australia. Australia is an island continent in the southern part of the world. Large forests grow along the east and west coasts. These forests are made up of **eucalyptus** trees. Koalas live mainly in the eucalyptus forests along the coasts of the eastern states—Victoria, New South Wales, and Queensland.

Kinds of koalas

There are three types of koalas: the Victoria koala, the New South Wales koala, and the Queensland koala. They are named after the states in which they live.

*Australia is located in the **southern hemisphere**, which means it is south of the equator. In this part of the world, the weather is warmer in the north than it is in the south because the north is closer to the equator.*

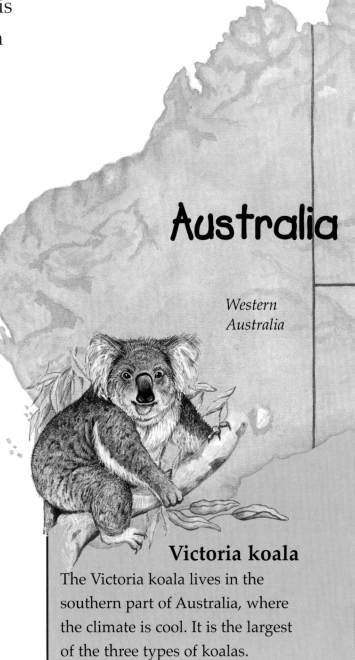

Australia

Western Australia

Victoria koala

The Victoria koala lives in the southern part of Australia, where the climate is cool. It is the largest of the three types of koalas.

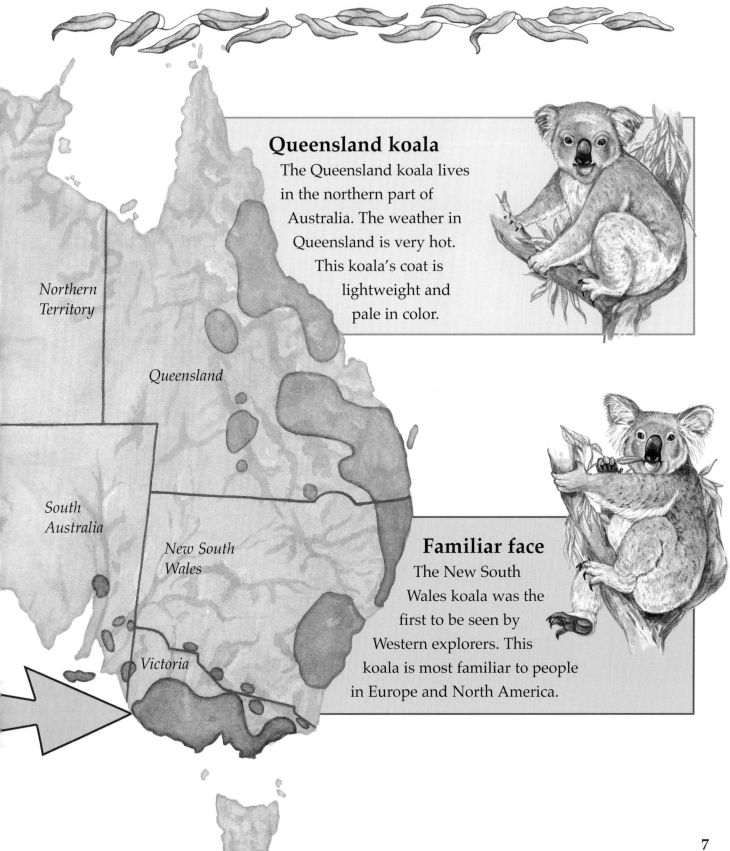

Queensland koala

The Queensland koala lives in the northern part of Australia. The weather in Queensland is very hot. This koala's coat is lightweight and pale in color.

Northern
Territory

Queensland

South
Australia

New South
Wales

Victoria

Familiar face

The New South Wales koala was the first to be seen by Western explorers. This koala is most familiar to people in Europe and North America.

What is a life cycle?

Every animal goes through a **life cycle**. A life cycle is made up of all the changes that happen to an animal from the time it is born until it becomes an adult that can make babies of its own. With each new baby, the life cycle starts again.

An animal's **life span** is different from its life cycle. A life span is the amount of time an animal is alive. Most koalas live fewer than ten years.

An early start

A marsupial's life cycle is made up of the same set of **stages**, or changes, as the life cycle of every other mammal. A mammal is born, grows, and becomes an adult. The birth of a **joey**, or marsupial baby, is different from that of other mammals, however. A joey is born while it is still an **embryo**, or developing baby, and continues to grow inside its mother's pouch. Other mammals finish developing into babies before they are born.

The life cycle of a koala

A tiny newborn koala lives and grows inside its mother's pouch. By the time it is six months old, the joey has eyes, ears, and fur. It crawls in and out of the pouch.

The koala is fully grown at the age of one year, but it is still young and stays with its mother. When it is three years old, the koala is an adult. It is now ready to have babies and start a new life cycle.

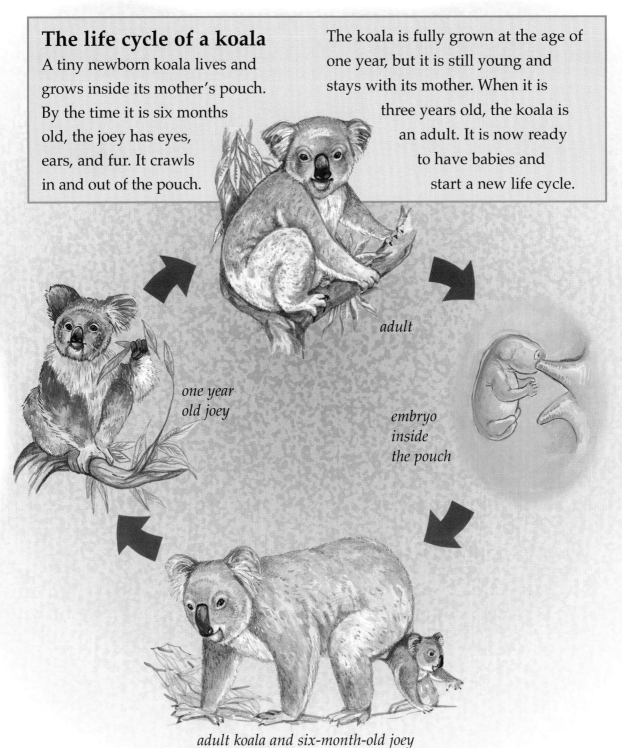

adult

one year old joey

embryo inside the pouch

adult koala and six-month-old joey

Journey to the pouch

Koalas **mate**, or make babies, in the spring and summer. About 35 days after mating, a female gives birth to a tiny joey. The joey is only about 0.8 of an inch (2 cm) long, it has no fur, and its eyes and ears are not formed. As soon as it is born, the joey knows by **instinct** that it must find its mother's pouch.

The trip across the mother's body is difficult! The joey cannot see or hear, and its back legs have not yet grown. It uses only its front legs to pull itself across its mother's belly. The joey has an excellent sense of smell. It can smell milk in the pouch. It finds the pouch by following the scent of the milk.

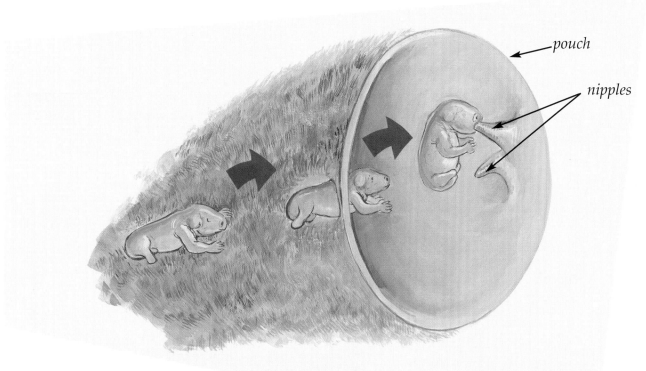

pouch

nipples

*For several months, the joey **nurses**, or drinks milk, inside its mother's pouch.*

Food to grow

As soon as the joey crawls inside the pouch, it begins sucking on a nipple. The nipple swells inside the baby's mouth so that the joey cannot let go or fall off when its mother moves around. The milk it drinks gives the joey the **nutrients**, or nourishment, it needs to grow.

An embryo is tiny, hairless, and helpless. It cannot live without milk from its mother's body.

A warm, safe place

The joey grows inside its mother's pouch for the first six months of its life. The pouch is a warm, cosy place for the baby koala. It also keeps the joey safe from **predators**.

Keeping the joey inside

A mother koala has a special muscle that keeps the pouch tightly closed, so the baby cannot fall out. By carrying her baby in the pouch, the mother can use her arms to climb trees.

A koala's pouch opens at the bottom, not at the top as a kangaroo's pouch does. This joey is peeking out from its mother's pouch.

11

Life with Mom

When a joey is six months old, it begins to spend short periods of time outside the pouch. By this time, it is about eight inches (20 cm) long. The joey's body is completely formed, but it is still growing. Now, instead of nursing inside the pouch, the joey lies on its mother's stomach to feed.

New food

Between six and seven months of age, the joey starts to eat another type of food, called **pap**, in addition to its mother's milk. Pap is produced by the mother's body as droppings. It contains partially digested eucalyptus leaves. The joey leans out of the rear-opening pouch to lick the pap. Pap is an important food for joeys.

Getting used to leaves

Eating pap helps a joey's body get used to eucalyptus leaves. Pap contains **microorganisms**, or tiny living things, which stay in the joey's stomach and help break down the tough leaves. When it is ready, the joey will stop drinking milk and start eating only eucalyptus leaves.

Riding around

As the joey gets older, it spends less time in the pouch, but it does not let go of its mother. It rides on her back or chest while she climbs, eats, and sleeps. Sometimes the mother holds onto the joey, but more often, the joey clings to her with its arms and legs.

Younger joeys cling to their mothers' chests, and older joeys ride on their mothers' backs.

Growing up

When a joey is about a year old, it gradually stops eating pap and drinking its mother's milk. It starts to eat only eucalyptus leaves. As it grows bigger, the joey learns to climb trees and find food on its own. It is almost an adult.

A one-year-old koala can live on its own, but it rarely does. Most young koalas stay with their mothers until they are two or three years old. A mother and her joey are the only koalas that live together and share the same tree.

The joey on the right is now able to live on eucalyptus leaves. It no longer nurses or eats pap.

This joey is getting better at climbing trees.

This growing joey still takes a ride on its mother's back from time to time.

Home on the range

A joey stays with its mother until it is about two years old. Then it must set out to find its own home range.

Each koala has its own territory, or home range. A home range contains between 15 and 20 trees. The trees in a range provide food and shelter for a koala. Koalas live by themselves in their home ranges, but they are not completely alone. They communicate with other koalas in nearby ranges.

"Out of my tree!"

Koalas are able to tell the difference between their trees and those of other koalas, but humans cannot. Koalas use scent and claw scratches to mark their trees. They are very possessive! Even after a koala dies, other koalas will wait almost a year before taking over its territory. It takes many months for the scent and claw marks to fade.

Trees for life

Trees are the most important part of a koala's home range. Some trees provide food, and others provide homes. When people cut down trees, they change a koala's home range. The koala cannot simply pick another tree. It needs specific kinds of trees for food, and it also has to respect the territories of other koalas.

A koala that is removed from its range will travel many miles to get back to its home.

Finding a mate

Adult males weigh between 18 and 31 pounds (8-14 kg). Females are smaller and weigh between 13 and 24 pounds (6-11 kg).

A female koala usually mates every other year. She does not mate if she has a joey that is less than a year old with her in her home range.

When female koalas reach three years of age, they are ready to mate, or make babies. Mating season is from September to March. During this time, male koalas compete with one another to attract mates. They bark, grunt, and even fight to get the attention of female koalas.

"Hey, look at me!"

A male koala makes a lot of noise so that females will notice him. He bellows loudly from the treetops so that nearby females will come closer to find out what all the racket is about. The call is so loud that it can be heard up to a half mile (0.8 km) away. The sound also warns competing males to stay away. A female koala makes a high-pitched sound to call to her mate.

Neighbors

A male koala's home range often overlaps with the home ranges of a few female koalas. If there are no females nearby, a male must travel on the ground to find one. The trip can be risky! (See page 27.)

The cycle starts again

After mating, male and female koalas return to their own home ranges. The male does not help raise the baby. The mother feeds and protects it. With each new joey, another life cycle begins.

scent gland

During the mating season, a male koala rubs his chest against the tree in which he lives. A **gland** *on his chest produces a smelly oil that tells other male koalas to stay away.*

Koalas love leaves!

An adult koala is a **folivore**, or leaf-eater. It eats eucalyptus leaves. Koalas are very picky about their food! Over 600 types of eucalyptus trees grow in Australia, but a koala will eat the leaves of only two or three kinds. It occasionally eats leaves from other trees as well, such as tea and cherry trees. Not all koalas like the same kinds of leaves. A koala's taste depends partly on where it lives. Each koala has its own favorite local trees from which it eats.

*Every now and then, a koala licks the ground. It is trying to get salt and **minerals** from the soil. There are few minerals in eucalyptus leaves.*

Poisonous food

All eucalyptus leaves contain poison, but some have more than others. Koalas sniff each leaf and inspect it carefully before eating it. They can tell which leaves are the most poisonous and avoid them.

Tough eaters

Eating eucalyptus leaves would kill most animals, but a koala can eat them without getting sick. It uses its strong jaws and ridged teeth to chew the leaves slowly and break them down as much as possible. The leaves then pass through a koala's special **digestive system**, which takes out the poisons. Eucalyptus leaves contain few nutrients, so a koala must eat about a pound (500 g) of leaves per day in order to stay healthy.

Koalas get the water they need from the leaves they eat. When there is not enough water in the leaves, koalas must find water to drink.

A koala's body

Koalas are built for climbing trees. Strong muscles in their legs and shoulders help them move among the branches without slipping. Koalas are able to scamper quickly up trees by grasping the trunks with both front paws and then pulling up their hind legs.

Perfect paws

Koalas have four things that help them climb trees easily—their paws! A koala has two "thumbs" on each of its front paws and one on each hind paw. These thumbs and the rough pads

front paw

on its palms help the koala

hind paw

get a firm grip on branches. Sharp claws on each toe dig into tree bark and keep the koala from sliding down the tree.

On the move

Koalas are good climbers, but they move awkwardly on the ground. They can run quickly if they have to, but they usually walk at a slow pace. Koalas are also able to swim.

Warm and dry

Koalas do not hide in shelters when the weather turns harsh. They have thick fur that helps keep them warm. The hairs of the fur grow very close together so the skin underneath stays dry.

This koala's longer fur protects it against the wind.

Comfortable seats

Koalas have thick, brownish gray fur to help protect them from rain and wind. The fur on a koala's bottom is extra thick to create a "cushion" that provides a comfortable seat when a koala is resting. The cushion fur has spots that camouflage the koala's bottom. It is difficult to see a koala when you look up into a tree.

Koala senses

A koala relies mostly on its senses of smell and hearing. With its sense of smell, it can find and choose eucalyptus leaves to eat. A koala's strong sense of hearing helps it keep in touch with other koalas.

The nose knows

A koala's nose is very large because its sense of smell is its most important sense. Before it will taste a eucalyptus leaf, the koala sniffs it to be certain that it is safe to eat. The koala also uses its sense of smell to keep track of other koalas.

Cheers, big ears

Koalas live far apart, so they need to be able to hear well in order to communicate with one another. Koalas scream when they are threatened and wail when they are hurt.

What little eyes you have!

Koalas have small eyes. They do not need very good vision because they do not have to watch out for predators when they are in the trees. Since they eat leaves instead of animals, they do not need good vision for hunting, either.

What do koalas do all day?

Koalas spend 16 to 20 hours of every day sleeping or resting! They sleep a lot because their diet gives them very little **energy**. They use less energy when they sleep than they do when they are awake. By sleeping often, koalas save their energy for finding food, climbing trees, grooming themselves, and caring for joeys.

Life in the trees

Koalas come down to the ground as little as possible. They spend all their time high in the treetops. If they need to move from one tree to another, they jump!

Beating the heat

In hot weather, koalas move from one branch to another to find a breeze. To cool off, they rest in the shady fork of a tree or lie with their arms and legs dangling in the air. At night, when it is cooler, koalas climb higher to search for food. If the air is cold, koalas curl up— just as you do when you are chilly!

Male koalas often come down from their trees to find mates. On the ground, they face many dangers. More koalas are killed during their mating season than at any other time.

Life with fewer trees

When people cut down trees, they leave gaps in a koala's home range. If the spaces between the trees are too large, the koala cannot jump to the next tree. It must climb down and walk across the gap. When a road is built through a koala's home range, the koala must try to cross it to reach the trees on the other side.

Owls, eagles, dingoes, and pythons may attack young koalas if they wander from their mothers.

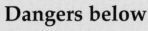

Dangers below

Koalas are slow-moving animals. Being on the ground can be dangerous for them because they cannot run fast enough to escape predators such as dingoes. Dogs that live in neighborhoods near koala ranges may chase or attack koalas. Some koalas are hit by cars when they cross a road to get from tree to tree.

Dangers to koalas

The greatest danger to koalas is the destruction of their **habitat**. Since settlers arrived in Australia, koalas have lost 80 percent of their habitat. People cut down eucalyptus trees to make room for houses, shopping malls, golf courses, and roads.

Land in demand

Eucalyptus trees that grow in rich soil have the most nutritious leaves for koalas. Rich soil is also needed by farmers and ranchers to raise crops and livestock. The farmers and ranchers cut down large areas of forest to use the soil. Without trees growing in it, the soil's quality is reduced, and the farmers soon have to clear more land for growing crops and raising animals. When the land is cleared, koalas lose their habitat.

No leaves left

Smaller forests force more koalas to eat from the same few trees. The koalas cannot help but **overgraze**, or eat all the leaves before new ones can grow. Before long, the koalas are out of food.

People are trying to find ways to preserve eucalyptus forests while making room for farming, ranching, and expanding cities.

Save the koalas!

Koalas are not **endangered**, but the loss of their habitat is a serious threat. Preserving koala habitats is the most important thing people can do to help these animals. Groups such as the Australian Koala Foundation (AKF) help protect koalas by working with governments to make laws that conserve koala's homes.

Safe outside the forest

Koala sanctuaries, such as the Lone Pine Koala Sanctuary on the western coast of Australia, are reserves where people raise and protect koalas. Researchers study koalas to find ways to protect them. You can do your own research about koalas on the Internet. Start your search at www.savethekoalas.com.

Learning about animals helps us respect all living things. No matter where we live, we can help save koalas and other animals around the world.

Glossary

communicate To pass along information through sounds and signs

digestive system The system in the body that breaks down food

embryo A developing baby

endangered Describing an animal species that is in danger of dying out

energy The power animals need to do work, such as moving and eating

eucalyptus A tall evergreen tree or shrub that grows in warm climates

gland A body part that produces and releases liquid

habitat The natural place where a plant or animal is found

home range An area in which an individual koala lives

instinct An animal's knowledge of how and when to do something without being taught

joey A marsupial baby

mammal A warm-blooded animal with a backbone and hair or fur that feeds on its mother's milk as an infant

marsupial A type of mammal that is born at a very early stage of development and finishes growing inside its mother's pouch

mate (v) To join together to make babies; (n) a mating partner

mineral A crystal in the soil that is nourishing to plants and animals

pap Special droppings that a joey eats

predator An animal that hunts and eats other animals

Index

1 2 3 4 5 6 7 8 9 0 Printed in the U.S.A. 1 0 9 8 7 6 5 4 3 2